I0148087

THE DEATH OF
BILLY THE KID

THE DEATH OF
BILLY THE KID

by
John William Poe
1933

New Foreword
by
Marc Simmons

SOUTHWEST HERITAGE SERIES

SUNSTONE
PRESS

SANTA FE

New Material © 2006 by Sunstone Press. All Rights Reserved.

No part of this book may be reproduced in any form or by any electronic or mechanical means including information storage and retrieval systems without permission in writing from the publisher, except by a reviewer who may quote brief passages in a review.

Sunstone books may be purchased for educational, business, or sales promotional use. For information please write: Special Markets Department, Sunstone Press, P.O. Box 2321, Santa Fe, New Mexico 87504-2321.

Library of Congress Cataloging-in-Publication Data:

Poe, John William, 1850-1923.
The death of Billy the Kid / by John William Poe ; new foreword by Marc Simmons.
   p. cm. -- (Southwest heritage series)
Originally published: Boston : Houghton Mifflin, 1933.
ISBN 0-86534-532-5 (softcover : alk. paper)
1. Billy, the Kid--Death and burial. 2. Outlaws--Southwest, New--Biography.
3. Poe, John William, 1850-1923. 4. Peace officers--Southwest, New--Biography.
5. Southwest, New--History--1848- 6. Frontier and pioneer life--Southwest, New.
I. Title. II. Series.

F786.B54P64 2006
364.15'52092--dc22
[B]

2006017896

Published in

WWW.SUNSTONEPRESS.COM
SUNSTONE PRESS / POST OFFICE BOX 2321 / SANTA FE, NM 87504-2321 /USA
(505) 988-4418 / ORDERS ONLY (800) 243-5644 / FAX (505) 988-1025

The Southwest Heritage Series is dedicated
to Jody Ellis and Marcia Muth Miller,
the founders of Sunstone Press,
whose original purpose and vision continues
to inspire and motivate our publications.

CONTENTS

I

THE SOUTHWEST HERITAGE SERIES

The history of the United States is written in hundreds of regional histories and literary works. Those letters, essays, memoirs, biographies and even collections of fiction are often first-hand accounts by people who wanted to memorialize an event, a person or simply record for posterity the concerns and issues of the times. Many of these accounts have been lost, destroyed or overlooked. Some are in private or public collections but deemed to be in too fragile condition to permit handling by contemporary readers and researchers.

However, now with the application of twenty-first century technology, nineteenth and twentieth century material can be reprinted and made accessible to the general public. These early writings are the DNA of our history and culture and are essential to understanding the present in terms of the past.

The Southwest Heritage Series is a form of literary preservation. Heritage by definition implies legacy and these early works are our legacy from those who have gone before us. To properly present and preserve that legacy, no changes in style or contents have been made. The material reprinted stands on its own as it first appeared. The point of view is that of the author and the era in which he or she lived. We would not expect photographs of people from the past to be re-imaged with modern clothes, hair styles and backgrounds. We should not, therefore, expect their ideas and personal philosophies to reflect our modern concepts.

Remember, reading their words and sharing their thoughts is a passport back into understanding how the past was shaped and how it influenced today's world.

Our hope is that new access to these older books will provide readers with a challenging and exciting experience.

II

FOREWORD TO THIS EDITION
by
Marc Simmons

If thirty-year-old John William Poe had not been present on the evening of July 14, 1881 when his boss Sheriff Pat Garrett killed Billy the Kid at Fort Sumner, New Mexico, then Poe would have missed his main chance to be remembered by history. As it was, he earned a niche in the annals of the Old West by participating in one of the most publicized incidents on the Southwestern frontier.

Raised on the family tobacco farm in Kentucky, John Poe struck out on his own in 1870, nearing the age of twenty, and headed west to find his destiny. A string of hard labor jobs, including that of a buffalo hunter on the plains of west Texas, seasoned the lad and provided experience useful for his next calling, in law enforcement.

Poe first served as a deputy U.S. marshal in Shackelford County, Texas and then in 1879 he became deputy sheriff of Wheeler County in the Panhandle. At the end of the following year, The Canadian River Cattlemen's Association hired Poe to serve as their representative and join New Mexico lawmen in tracking down Billy the Kid, whose livestock rustling had long proved costly to Texas ranchers. John Poe's own account of what followed, incorporating the sensational slaying of Billy the Kid, forms the subject of this book.

John Poe during that episode received an appointment as a special deputy sheriff of Lincoln County, New Mexico even while he remained in service to the Cattlemen's Association. Gaining a reputation for honesty and fair play, he was able to win election as sheriff upon retirement of Pat Garrett in 1882. A year later he married Sophie Alberding, a native of California who had been living with the pioneer Lea family in Roswell on the Pecos River.

Thereafter, "John William," as his wife Sophie always called him, finished up his career as a law officer, ranched for a time near Fort Stanton, and spent the last decades of his life as a Roswell business man, banker, and a regent of the prestigious New Mexico Military Institute. A photographic portrait of him in those years shows a distinguished gentleman, fashionably dressed and properly groomed—a far cry from his rough early-day appearance as a buffalo hunter. John W. Poe died at Roswell in 1923, a man who had lived in two worlds.

Understandably, Mr. Poe late in life was sought out by scholars, popular writers, and others seeking knowledge concerning the killing of the Kid. He finally committed to paper his recollections on that subject and turned the short manuscript over to his wife for safe-keeping.

The Death of Billy the Kid first appeared in print in magazine format (1919). Noted western author E. A. Brininstool privately printed the text as "a brochure" in 1922 and again in 1923. Houghton Mifflin Company of Boston brought out the first edition in book form with hard covers and illustrations in 1933. It contains a lengthy and still valuable introduction by Colonel Maurice Garland Fulton (1877–1955), an English professor at the New Mexico Military Institute. The cadets affectionately called him "Pappy."

Based on his reputation as a scholar of the Lincoln County War, Sophie Poe had urged that Colonel Fulton be enlisted to write the introduction for *The Death of Billy the Kid*. Although an abundance of new material has surfaced since he composed the introductory essay, his summary of events, therein, that led up to Billy's death provides modern readers with enough background to place Poe's narrative in proper perspective.

The Death of Billy the Kid has been out of print for decades. Interest in the young outlaw's career continues unabated, so that this new 1933 facsimile reprint of John W. Poe's book should find an eager readership.

Finally, it should be noted that Sophie A. Poe published her husband's biography and her own autobiography in the book *Buckboard Days* (1936 and reprint edition 1981). In it her personal courage and endurance shine through. The volume is now regarded as an important part of the literature and history of the American West.

Without question, *The Death of Billy the Kid* stands as a worthy addition to Sunstone Press's Southwest Heritage Series.

III

FACSIMILE OF 1933 EDITION

WILLIAM H. BONNEY
Alias Billy the Kid

THE DEATH OF
BILLY THE KID

BY
JOHN W. POE
Deputy Sheriff under Pat Garrett
Present at the Killing

WITH AN INTRODUCTION BY
MAURICE GARLAND FULTON

and with illustrations

Boston and New York
HOUGHTON MIFFLIN COMPANY
The Riverside Press Cambridge
1933

The Riverside Press
CAMBRIDGE · MASSACHUSETTS
PRINTED IN THE U.S.A.

ILLUSTRATIONS

INTRODUCTION

IN A straightforward, plain, and mat-
ter-of-fact style that adds sincerity to
the recital, the late John W. Poe has
recorded fully the circumstances of
the death of Billy the Kid. His
knowledge was first-hand, for he was
one of the posse of three who, in the
midsummer of 1881, very unexpect-
edly, both to themselves and everyone else, gave New Mexico and the
Texas Panhandle everlasting riddance
from that young scapegrace. Though
the account was not written until
nearly thirty-five years later, Mr.
Poe's undimmed memory and love of

Introduction

exact statement make the narrative fully as trustworthy as if written immediately after the event.

To one like myself, who saw Mr. Poe but casually in the tranquillity of 1922–23, the last year of his somewhat more than threescore and ten, there was little to suggest how largely the earlier half of his life had been filled with frontier hardships and dangers. The large, broad-shouldered physique, together with an impressive gravity of demeanor, betokened that the man sitting at the president's desk of the Citizens' National Bank of Roswell, New Mexico, was a person of consequence, possibly of great courage and determination, but did not

Introduction

give the passer-by an inkling of the rôles he had played in ushering in law and order upon the raw and raucous Southwestern frontier.

At the urge of an adventurous spirit, Mr. Poe had left his boyhood home on a Kentucky farm at seventeen, and 'gone West.' By the spring of 1871 he had penetrated into Kansas and was then at the end of the Santa Fe Railroad, then slightly below Emporia, making a livelihood as a member of a construction crew. In 1872, he was a step farther into the unsettled parts, cutting timber and cross-ties on Red River in Texas and the Indian Territory. In the spring of 1872, he pulled up stakes and

Introduction

traveled horseback two hundred and fifty miles farther west to Fort Griffin, then almost the *ultima thule* of the frontier. Here he handled a large wood contract for the garrison, but when this was completed, he became one of the crowd of buffalo-hunters who were swarming over the plains of West Texas. In the four years (1874–1878) spent on the buffalo range, Mr. Poe made a reputation as one of the most successful hunters. His estimate that he had killed in the neighborhood of twenty thousand buffalo with his own Sharps suggests both his skill and the lucrativeness of the business.

When buffalo-hunting ceased to be

Introduction

profitable, Mr. Poe entered upon several years of service as law-enforcement officer by accepting appointment as town marshal for Fort Griffin. In this capacity he served but one year, long enough, however, to show his remarkable qualifications. He held a tight rein on that very tough and cosmopolite town without killing a single person. Such a record won him higher recognition in 1879, when he became a deputy United States Marshal. He was at once stationed at Fort Elliott in the northeast corner of the Texas Panhandle, then in the throes of the bold, reckless life incident to its first settlement. Cattle-stealing was rampant, but Mr. Poe

Introduction

curbed it so markedly that the Canadian River Cattlemen's Association selected him to look especially after their interests. How this employment led to a special mission into New Mexico, Mr. Poe relates at the beginning of his story.

It will clarify matters somewhat, however, if we understand how Billy the Kid, the particular thorn in the flesh of the Panhandle cattlemen whom Mr. Poe was commissioned to remove, had developed. The limits of an introduction forbid a full-length account of William Bonney, *alias* Kid, *alias* William Antrim (to give the equipment of names under which he usually appears in legal

documents) who has nowadays become simply Billy the Kid. We cannot take space even to divest the first
stages of his career of the legendizing
that unquestionably envelops them;
nor can we chronicle his part in the
feud known as the Lincoln County
War. Suffice it to say that when
those disorders almost ceased in the
summer of 1878, he had taken a prom-
inent part in all the fighting, and
emerged with a reputation for cool-
ness and shooting skill that was remarkable for one just leaving behind
his teens. But the hand of the law
was clutching at him with two indictments — one for the killing of
Sheriff William Brady, the other for

Introduction

the killing of his deputy, George
Hindman, an outrageous deed which
Billy the Kid and five or six others
of his clique had accomplished on
April 1, 1878.

The defeated remnant of the Mc-
Sween faction, including Billy the
Kid, withdrew to Fort Sumner, about
ninety miles northeast of Lincoln.
This old army establishment was now
shorn of the prestige it had possessed
ten years before, when the Bosque
Redondo experiment was in progress,
seeking to impound and civilize the
several thousand Navajos and Mes-
calero Apaches on the large reserva-
tion established on the Rio Pecos.
The remains of the fort, including

Introduction

several square miles of land and a
collection of buildings originally built
by the United States Government
for officers' quarters, barracks, store-
houses, stables, and outhouses, had
been purchased by Lucien B. Maxwell, of Maxwell Land Grant fame,
who, after the loss of his vast estate
on the Cimarron, had moved into
the southern part of the Territory in
an effort to recoup his fortune. In
the course of time, Lucien B. Maxwell had been gathered to his fathers,
but his son Pedro, more commonly
called Pete, had succeeded to the
headship of the family and the man-
agement of the sheep and cattle interests.

Introduction

During the sojourn at Fort Sumner,
Billy the Kid came into friendship
with the Maxwells. The family seems
to have been largely feminine, and
Billy the Kid's personality and career
had elements which made him at-
tractive to that sex. Mrs. Maxwell,
her daughters, and even the old Na-
vajo servant-woman, Dulivena, grew
attached to him, and welcomed his
presence whenever he was near Fort
Sumner. It is still a moot question
whether there developed between the
young outlaw and one of the Maxwell
daughters any more lively degree of
interest than friendly acquaintance,
but the present writer himself dis-
counts heavily the echoes of the old

gossip that may still be heard or found in print.

During the late summer and early fall of 1878, Lincoln County was in perhaps a worse state than when the Lincoln County War was in active progress. Instead of simply two warring factions, several bands of outlaws were roaming at will and harrying the land and its inhabitants. During all this pellmell havoc and confusion, Billy the Kid began to emerge more and more as what, in present-day parlance, would be called a 'public enemy.' He came back into Lincoln on several occasions, accompanied by some of his former McSween adherents, and stole horses, which they carried into the Panhandle to sell. On one such foray, the clerk at the Indian Agency, Bernstein, was killed, and while Billy the Kid was not actually responsible, yet it was generally ascribed to him and became the basis for issuing a United States warrant for him.

In October the new governor, General Lew Wallace, came to New Mexico, clothed with plenipotentiary power to quiet the disorders. His program at first was all for mild measures. So far as old offenders were concerned, he would wipe the slate clean at once. In November he issued an amnesty proclamation extending a general pardon to both

Introduction

factions for what had been done between February and November, 1878,
but with the proviso that the terms
of this offer might not be taken ad-
vantage of by 'any person in bar
of conviction under indictment now
found and returned for any such
crimes and misdemeanors.' This lim-
itation shut the door upon the Kid,
under a double indictment for the
killing of Brady and Hindman. He
probably was not highly uncomfort-
able under the situation, for the officers of the law had virtually given
over their attempts to arrest him.
The fall term of court had been pre-
termitted, and this created a lapse of
several months before there would be

any activity on the part of those charged with arresting offenders or dispensing justice.

By February, 1879, the two original factions were ready to patch up a peace, and a conference was held in Lincoln. Billy the Kid, Tom O'Folliard, and probably one of the Salazars, representing the former McSween group, and Jesse Evans, Tom Campbell, and James J. Dolan, representing the former Murphy-Dolan-Riley contingent, met and drew up terms of peace. But hardly was the ink dry on the document when the feud flared up again. As the conferees and several of their friends were going down the street of Lin-

Introduction

coln celebrating the newly established era of amity and good-will, they encountered Huston J. Chapman, a lawyer of the trouble-making type whom Mrs. McSween had secured to look after her interests. For three or four months he had been a veritable gadfly both to the Dolan faction and to the military at Fort Stanton, especially Colonel Nathan A. M. Dudley, the commanding officer, who had come to the rescue of the Dolan crowd when they were hard pressed toward the end of the five-days fight at Lincoln in July. There was a clash of words between the Dolan group and Chapman, followed by two shots which left the lawyer's body lifeless on the streets. If the old indictments mean anything, Campbell and Dolan were considered the principals in this killing, while Jesse Evans was an accessory.

BILLY THE KID.

$500 REWARD.

I will pay $500 reward to any person or persons who will capture William Bonny, alias The Kid, and deliver him to any sheriff of New Mexico. Satisfactory proofs of identity will be required.

LEW. WALLACE,
Governor of New Mexico.

Governor Wallace felt that the Chapman killing indicated a new and possibly more serious outbreak than before. He came upon the scene and took personal charge of the arrest of those responsible for the murder. One of the first his mind

[xxii]

turned toward was Billy the Kid, and
the letter to Colonel Edward Hatch,
then commanding the troops in New
Mexico, was short and pointed:

I have just ascertained that the Kid
is at a place called Las Tablas, a plazita
up near Coghlin's ranch. He has with
him Thomas O'Folliard, and was going
out of the Territory, but stopped there
to rest his horses, saying he would stay a
few days. He was at the house of one
Salazar.

You will oblige me by sending a de-
tachment after the two men; and if they
are caught, send them on to Fort Stanton
for trial as accessories to the murder of
Chapman.

If the men are found to have left Las
Tablas, I beg they may be pursued until
caught. The details are commended to
your good judgment.

News of the Governor's determina-

Introduction

tion must have reached Billy the Kid, for, as the following letter to Governor Wallace, written a few days later, shows, he sought to bespeak for himself some sort of special dispensation:

I have heard that you will give one thousand ($) for my body, which as I can understand it means alive as a witness. I know it is as a witness against those that murdered Mr. Chapman. If it was so as I could appear at court, I could give the desired information, but I have indictments against me for things that happened in the Lincoln County War, and am afraid to give myself up because my enemies would kill me. The day Mr. Chapman was murdered, I was in Lincoln at the request of good citizens to meet Mr. J. J. Dolan, to meet as a friend so as to be able to lay aside our arms and go to work. I was present when

Introduction

Mr. Chapman was murdered and know
who did it; and if it were not for those
indictments, I would have made it clear
before now. If it is in your power to annul
those indictments, I hope you will do so,
so as to give me a chance to explain.
Please send me an answer telling me
what you can do. You can send answer
by bearer. I have no wish to fight any
more; indeed, I have not raised an arm
since your proclamation. As to my character I refer you to any of the citizens, for
the majority of them are my friends and
have been helping me all they could. I
am called Kid Antrim, but Antrim is my
stepfather's name.

Waiting an answer I remain,
Your obedient servant
W. H. BONNEY[1]

Negotiations, both by letters and

[1] This letter is preserved in the archives of the
Wallace family. I am enabled to publish it through
the courtesy of Mr. Lew Wallace, Jr., of New
York City. The spelling and punctuation have
been slightly improved.

Introduction

by interview, finally brought the Governor and the young outlaw into an understanding by which Billy the Kid was to undergo pseudo-arrest by Sheriff Kimbrell. The program was carried out, and Billy the Kid lodged under guard in the Patron Store building in Lincoln, pending the approaching session of the grand jury. When court convened about the middle of April, he was one of the witnesses whose testimony resulted in the indictment of Dolan, Campbell, and Jesse Evans in connection with the Chapman killing. The Kid himself appeared in court and pleaded not guilty to the indictments against him for the Brady-Hindman killing. A

Introduction

change of venue to Doña Ana County
was allowed, an arrangement which
postponed his trial a month or two.

In the interval, however, Billy the
Kid suffered a change of heart. Just
before time to be taken over to La
Mesilla for trial, he escaped and took
refuge at Fort Sumner. Why he did
this is hard to determine now. Possibly his faith weakened in regard to
Governor Wallace's ability to guar-
antee immunity, especially when the
district judge, Warren Bristol, and the
district attorney, William L. Ryner-
son, were implacably hostile to the
McSween faction as well as politically
opposed to Governor Wallace. Probably he also realized that if he did

Introduction

happen to 'come clear' at the trial, he would face the enmity of the Dolan faction, embittered by his testimony before the grand jury. At any rate, he elected to burn his bridges behind him, and at once resumed his former habit of looking out for himself with the aid of his trusty firearms.

He was at large in the vicinity of Fort Sumner for approximately a year and a half. The question of a livelihood he met through monte-dealing and cattle-stealing. At the point of the pistol he had presented a claim to John S. Chisum for five hundred dollars back pay for services rendered during the Lincoln County War, but the wily old cattle baron denied the claim, and out-argued the Kid into lowering the revolver. The Kid, however, bestowed a parting threat that he would obtain the five hundred dollars in good measure from the Chisum herds, and he and his companions proceeded to make good the threat. Their cattle-stealing, however, soon passed the reprisal stage, and became a definitely organized business. His gang grew until it included, not only old Lincoln County associates like Charlie Bowdre and Tom O'Folliard, but also some even rougher men who had drifted into Fort Sumner, such as Dave Rudabaugh, Tom Pickett, and Billy Wilson. Even the community itself at

Introduction

Fort Sumner probably furnished some recruits.

Fort Sumner was advantageously located as a base for such a business. About forty miles east, in the vicinity of Las Portales Lake, was an ideal hide-out, where the booty might be concealed. It was easy to take horses out into the Panhandle and find a ready market at Tascosa and other settlements. It was equally easy to gather up on the return a bunch of cattle and carry them down through Fort Sumner and into Lincoln County, where Pat Coghlin at Tulerosa had a dépôt ready and waiting for stolen cattle, with which to fulfill his government contracts. It

Introduction

was some such system that brought
to a head the irritation of the Panhandle cattlemen. Frank Stewart, as
special agent, came over into New
Mexico with a posse in the early part
of December, 1880, to retake cattle
supposedly in the vicinity of Fort
Sumner and in the hands of Billy
the Kid's gang. But prior to this the
toils had begun to close around
the Kid. As Sheriff-elect of Lincoln
County, Pat Garrett had already
begun his stern pursuit of the Kid
and his followers. The Kid aggra-
vated the case against himself, when
in the latter part of November, 1880,
he killed a popular resident of White
Oaks, Jim Carlyle, in a fight at the

Introduction

Greathouse Ranch with a posse from White Oaks. Garrett carried the pursuit shortly afterward straight into Fort Sumner, in the vicinity of which the Kid's gang was hiding. Frank Stewart and his men from the Canadian joined forces with Garrett's posse. O'Folliard was killed by means of an ambush; a little later, the Kid, Rudabaugh, Bowdre, Tom Pickett, and Billy Wilson were rounded up in a small hut at Stinking Springs. Bowdre was killed, the hat he was wearing causing him to be mistaken for the Kid. The remaining four decided then on surrender.

The Kid was taken to Santa Fe, where he was kept in jail until April,

Introduction

1881, when he was taken down to La Mesilla for trial. This was quickly over, and the Kid sentenced by Judge Bristol to be hanged on May 13 at Lincoln. His dramatic escape is perhaps too well known to be given here at any greater length than in the words Garrett wrote on the order of execution:

I certify that I rec'd the within named William Bonney alias Kid alias William Antrim into my custody on the 21st day of April, A.D. 1881. And I further certify that on April 28th the said Wm. Bonney alias Kid alias William Antrim made his escape by killing his guard, J. W. Bell and Robert Olinger in Lincoln, Lincoln Co., New Mexico.

This exhibition of derring-do put Billy the Kid more on a pedestal than

Introduction

before and attracted toward him the
instinctive admiration of all lovers of
'the art of daring,' to use the phrase
of Mirabeau. Up to this point in
his career, opinion had been divided.
Was he a sneaks-by or a lad of met-
tle, a ruffian or a hero? — and no definite answer seemed possible. But
after this escape, popular imagina-
tion seized him for its darling, and
recognized in him more than a common killer and thief, more than a
common leech on society. Even the
Santa Fe New Mexican, always dis-
paraging of the Kid, bestowed a
grudging plaudit in the issues of
May 4, 1881, a few days after the
escape:

Introduction

The above [the account of Kid's escape] is the record of as bold a deed as those versed in the annals of crime can recall. It surpasses anything of which the Kid had been guilty, so far that his past offenses lose much of heinousness in comparison with it, and it effectually settles the question as to whether the Kid is a cowardly cut-throat or a thoroughly reckless and fearless man. Never before has he faced death boldly or run any great risk in the perpetration of his bloody deeds. Bob Olinger used to say that he was a cur, and that every man he had killed had been murdered in cold blood and without the slightest chance of defending himself. The Kid displayed no disposition to correct this until this last act of his when he taught Olinger by bitter experience that his theory was anything but correct.

But from such an Apollo, the Kid's life turns almost into the commonplace in its last scene. This

young outlaw, with a Territorial reward of five hundred dollars upon
his head, hides himself in the friendly
camp of a Mexican sheep-herder and
palters with the idea of leaving the
country, at least for a time. One
July night he seeks the sociability of a
baile at the home of one of the leading
Mexican ranch-owners in the vicinity
of Fort Sumner. After the dance ends
about eleven o'clock, he rides back
to the sheep camp of the Mexican
friend with whom he is hiding, and
then decides to go over to the Maxwell
ranch. About midnight he reaches
the room of one of the employees of
the Maxwells living in the long row
of adobe rooms to the south of the

building in which the Maxwell family lived.

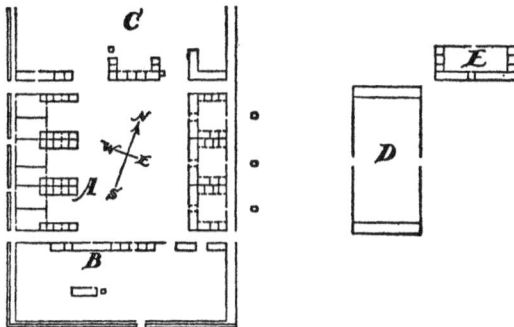

GROUND PLAN OF FORT SUMNER
A. Maxwell's house. B. Old quartermaster's store-house from one of the rooms in which the Kid went to Maxwell's to his death. C. Peach orchard. D. Corral. E. Old hospital where Bowdre's widow lived.

After divesting himself of shoes and garments superfluous on a July night to a man seeking relaxation, he grows hungry, and, learning that a freshly killed quarter of beef is hanging on

[xxxvii]

Introduction

the north porch of the Maxwell dwell-
ing, he sallies forth, butcher-knife in
hand, and *sans* shoes and shirt, across
the intervening yard, to cut for himself a piece of meat. His route takes
him past two members of the posse at
the end of the south porch, and at this
point he seems to lose that genius for
preserving his own life by means of
his flaming pistol which heretofore
had stood him in such good stead.
He moves on past the two strangers,
who must have been revealed fully
to him in the moonlight, and dodges
into the doorway of Pete Maxwell's
bedroom, there to confront the pistol
held by Pat Garrett and from it to
receive his *coup de grâce*.

Introduction

It was never easy to draw out Mr. Poe about the death of the Kid, but when he did relate the story, his listeners found it interesting and profitable hearing. At Mrs. Poe's urging, he finally wrote out the account and turned it over to her to keep against whatever time might be suitable for its publication. In the early part of 1919, Mr. Edward Seymour, of New York, a gentleman interested in the history of the West, feeling skeptical about certain information regarding the death of the Kid which had come to him, inquired of the late Charles Goodnight as to a reliable source of information. Mr. Goodnight referred him to Mr. Poe, making the comment

Introduction

that 'whatever John Poe would furnish would be true.' As the easiest way of giving Mr. Seymour the facts, Mr. Poe sent him a copy of the account Mrs. Poe was treasuring. This eventually reached Mr. E. A. Brininstool, of Los Angeles, who, perceiving its value, secured its publication in an English magazine, *The Wide World,* for December, 1919. Afterward Mr. Brininstool published the account as a privately printed brochure, which in the course of time passed into the limbo of 'out of print.'

The present volume gives to this grim episode of the old Southwest that definitive and permanent form

THE CITIZENS NATIONAL BANK OF ROSWELL, N.M.

OFFICE OF THE PRESIDENT

JNO. W. POE,
PRESIDENT

Roswell, New Mexico,
March 5th, 1923.

Mr. E. A. Brininstool
1428 South Norton Ave,
Los Angeles, Cal,

Dear Mr. Brininstool:-

        I am in receipt of your favor of the 28th ult. and note what you say relative to a statement recently made by some person to the effect the "Billy the Kid" was killed in the spring of 1862.

        In reply I beg to state that whoever made such statement is entirely in error and is positively mistaken as to the time of that occurrance. Inasmuch as I was present and know positively whereof I speak, I believe you will readily understand that I am absolutely correct in this matter.

        The "Kid" was killed on the night of the 14th of July, 1881, and the only accurate and true account of his death and the circumstances leading up to and surrounding it is that which I gave you some three years ago.

        It seems too bad that people will continue to circulate erroneous and false stories about this occurrance but I suppose it is one of the things that will have to be endured.

        You are at liberty to use this letter in any way you may see fit or show it to any one who may be interested.

        With kind regards, I remain

        Yours very truly,

        Jno. W. Poe

(Facsimile published by courtesy of Mr. E. A. Brininstool)

Introduction

it richly merits, considering its importance as source material.

MAURICE GARLAND FULTON

The Death of Billy the Kid

THE DEATH
OF BILLY THE KID

THE EXIGENCY

DURING the winter of 1880–81 I was
living in the Panhandle of Texas,
where for some time previous I had
been serving as deputy U.S. marshal,
and also as deputy sheriff. About the
middle of that winter the cattlemen
of the Panhandle, who had organized an association for the protection
of their cattle interests known as the
Canadian River Cattle Association,
and of whom Mr. Charles Goodnight
was one of the leading spirits, submitted a proposition to me to enter

[3]

their employ, and, as their representative, to co-operate with the authorities
of New Mexico with the view of sup-
pressing and putting an end to the
wholesale raiding and stealing of
cattle, which had been and was then
carried on by Billy the Kid and his
gang of desperadoes, of whom there
were quite a number, and of whom
a great majority of the people in the
localities where they were operating
stood in fear and terror.

An agreement was arrived with the
above-mentioned cattlemen under
which I was given practically un-
limited authority to act for and re-
present them in all matters wherein
their interests were affected in New

The Death of Billy the Kid

Mexico, including authority to draw
for all funds necessary for apprehend-
ing and prosecuting thieves and rust-
lers generally, and particularly those
depredations of stock belonging to
the Association, the only restriction
being, of course, that I should pro-
ceed in a lawful manner.

Pursuant to this agreement, some
time in March, 1881, I went to
White Oaks, Lincoln County, New
Mexico, which place was at that time
quite a booming mining town, and
was a sort of rendezvous for tough
characters generally, including the
following of the Kid, their friends and
sympathizers, of whom there were
many. It was here that I first met

The Death of Billy the Kid

Pat Garrett, who was at that time sheriff of Lincoln County. After an interview with him, in which I explained the nature of my business in New Mexico, it was agreed that I should be commissioned as one of his deputies, which was done, and that we should co-operate in every way possible in an endeavor to suppress crime in that region generally, and particularly cattle rustling.

It should be remembered that, at this particular time, the Kid was lying in jail, or rather held under guard, at Lincoln, the county seat, under sentence of death for murder, but had many sympathizers in the country and a number of followers still at

JOHN W. POE   PAT F. GARRETT

The photographs show the two men as they appeared in 1881

large pursuing their trade of stealing cattle, committing robberies, and various other crimes, and that they were operating from the Panhandle of Texas through a great part of New Mexico and into Arizona.

At our first meeting it was agreed between Garrett and myself that I should make a trip to Tombstone, Arizona, which was then in its palmiest days as a mining camp, and where some of the stolen cattle from the Panhandle had been driven, which I hoped to recover, and that upon my return to White Oaks within a short time, we should meet again and confer together over the situation and decide upon what further course we were to pursue. This program was carried out, and on the day of our second meeting in White Oaks, some time during the month of April, information came from Lincoln, some forty miles distant, that Billy the Kid had escaped from his guards, killing two of them, and was again at large. This occurred only a few days before the time set for the Kid's execution, and naturally caused a great deal of excitement throughout that region, as well as some rejoicing on the part of his friends and sympathizers.

THE HUNT

Upon receipt of this information, Garrett immediately started for Lincoln, while it was agreed that I should remain on the lookout for the Kid at White Oaks for a time, as it was not known what direction he would take or where he would go after getting out of Lincoln.

Upon arriving at Lincoln on the night following the day of the escape, Garrett found that two of his deputies (Bob Olinger and a man named Bell) had been killed by the Kid, who, partly by means of a cunning ruse and partly by reason of the carelessness of the deputies, had broken into a room containing firearms, adjacent to where he was guarded, secured a six-shooter, by means of which he immediately pro-

ceeded to add two more to his already
long list of victims, and then had
compelled another man on the premises to secure a horse for him, upon
which he rode away, leaving the
people of the little town completely
terrorized.

Garrett at once organized several
posses and scoured the country in all
directions for several days in an endeavor to recapture his man, but,
failing to find any trace of him, finally
gave up the hunt in the full belief
that the Kid had gone to Old Mexico.
According to my recollection this
killing and escape occurred in the
latter part of April, after which we
were unable to learn anything what-

ever indicating the whereabouts of
the Kid until the July following, not-
withstanding the fact that we were
constantly on the alert and made
the most strenuous efforts to locate
him.

During the interval between the
time of the Kid's escape and the time
he was killed in July following, I con-
tinued to make headquarters at White
Oaks, during which time I scoured
the country thoroughly, finding many
stolen cattle, also hides of stolen cattle which had been slaughtered, belonging to the Association I was representing; had a number of arrests
made, prosecutions instituted, etc.,
being assisted in all this by Sheriff

The Death of Billy the Kid

Garrett, who co-operated with me in every way possible, and whom I found to be a very brave and efficient officer.

Some time in the early part of July following the happenings above related, I was approached by a man in White Oaks, whom I had formerly known in Texas, who, although addicted to habits of dissipation, was a man of good principles, and who had, on previous occasions, shown a desire to assist me in the work I had in hand.

This man told me a story in strict confidence — as he probably felt that his life depended on its being treated in that respect — the gist of which

The Death of Billy the Kid

was that, for want of a better place, he had for some time been occupying as sleeping quarters a vacant room in a certain livery stable, owned and operated by two men who were known to be friends of Billy the Kid; and that a short time previous, while in his sleeping quarters at night, he had overheard a conversation between the two men, which convinced him that the Kid was yet in the country, making his headquarters at Fort Sumner, about a hundred miles distant from White Oaks, and that he, at two different times since his escape from Lincoln, had been in the vicinity of White Oaks, and had met or communicated with the two men whose conversation he had over-heard.

I was somewhat skeptical as to the correctness of this information, as it seemed almost unbelievable that the Kid, after nearly three months had elapsed from the time of his escape with a price on his head, and under sentence of death, would still be lingering in the country. However, in view of the peculiar conditions then existing in the country, and the fact that the Kid had many friends and sympathizers who looked upon him as a hero and who would probably shelter and protect him, I came to the conclusion that there was possibly truth in the story which had been told me, and I immediately went to the county seat [Lincoln], where I laid the matter before the sheriff as it had been told me.

The sheriff was much more skeptical as to the truth of the story than I was — said he could not believe there was any truth in what the White Oaks man had told me. He finally said that, if I desired it, he would go to Roswell, where we would find one of his deputies named McKinney, and from there the three of us would go to Fort Sumner with the determination of unearthing the Kid if he were there. This was agreed upon, and the following day we went to Roswell, where we found McKinney, who expressed his disbelief in the White Oaks story, but who willingly joined us for the expedition to Fort Sumner, which place is some eighty miles distant from Roswell.

After a few hours spent in Roswell arranging for the trip, we started about sundown, riding out of town in a different direction from that we intended to travel later, as it was absolutely necessary to keep the public in ignorance of our plans if anything was to be accomplished. After we were well out of the settlement, we changed our course and rode in the direction of Fort Sumner until about midnight, when we stopped, picketed our horses, and slept on our saddle-blankets for the remainder of the night. The next day we rode some fifty or fifty-five miles, halting late in the evening at a point in the sand hills some five or six miles out from Fort Sumner, where we again picketed our horses and slept until morning.

RECONNOITERING FORT SUMNER

It was agreed that as I was not known in Fort Sumner, while the other two men were, Garrett having a year or two previously resided there, I should ride into the place with the object of reconnoitering the ground and gathering such information as was possible that might aid us in our purpose, while the other two men were to remain out of sight in the sand hills for the day, and in case of my failure to return to them before night, they were to meet me after darkness came on at a certain point agreed on some four miles out of Fort Sumner.

In pursuance of this plan, I next morning left my companions and rode into town, where I arrived about ten o'clock. Fort Sumner at that time had a population of only some two or three hundred people, nearly all of whom were natives or Mexicans, there being not more than one or two dozen Americans in the place, a majority of whom were tough or undesirable characters, in sympathy with the Kid, while the remainder stood in terror of him.

When I entered the town, I noticed that I was being watched from every side, and soon after I had stopped and hitched my horse in front of a store which had a saloon annex, a number of men gathered around and began to question me as to where I was from, where bound, etc. I answered with as plausible a yarn as I was able to give, telling them I was from White Oaks, where I had been engaged in mining, and was on my way to the Panhandle, where I had formerly lived.

This story seemed to allay their suspicions to some extent, and I was invited to join in a special drink at the saloon, which I did, being very careful that I absorbed but a very small portion of the liquor. This operation was repeated several times, as was the custom in those days, after which I went to a near-by restaurant for something to eat. After I had eaten a square meal, I loitered about the village for some three hours, chatting casually with people I met in the hope of learning something definite as to whether or not the Kid was there or had recently been there, but was unable to learn anything further than that the people with whom I conversed were still suspicious of me, and it was plain that many of them were on the alert, expecting something to happen. In fact, there was a very tense situation in Fort Sumner on that day, as the Kid was at that very time hiding in one of the natives' houses there, and if the object of my visit had become known, I should have stood no chance for my life whatever.

It was understood, when I left my companions in the morning, that in case of my being unable to learn any definite information in Fort Sumner, I was to go to the ranch of a Mr. Rudolph (an acquaintance and a supposed friend of Garrett's), which was located some seven miles north of Fort Sumner at a place called Sunnyside, with the purpose of securing from him, if possible, some information as to the whereabouts of the man we were after.

Accordingly, I started from Fort Sumner about the middle of the afternoon for Rudolph's ranch, arriving there some time before night. I found Mr. Rudolph at home, presented the letter of introduction which Garrett had given me, and told him that I wished to stop overnight with him. After reading the letter, he said that Garrett was a very good friend of his, and that he would be very glad to furnish me with accommodations for the night, invited me into his house, took charge of my horse, etc.

The Death of Billy the Kid

After supper was over, I engaged
in conversation with him, discussing
the conditions in the country generally, and after some little time, I
led up to the escape of Billy the Kid
from Lincoln, and remarked that I
had heard a report that the Kid was
hiding in or about Fort Sumner.
Upon my making this remark, the
old gentleman showed plainly that
he was getting nervous; said he had
heard that such a report was about,
but did not believe it, as the Kid was
in his opinion too shrewd to be caught
lingering in that part of the country
with a price upon his head and know-
ing that the officers of the law were
diligently seeking him.

The Death of Billy the Kid

By this time I was pretty well convinced that Mr. Rudolph was naturally well-intentioned, but like so many others, was in almost mortal terror of the Kid, and on account of this fear, was very reluctant to say anything whatever about him. I then told him plainly the object of our errand — that I had come to him with the express purpose of learning, if possible, where the Kid could be found; that we believed he was hiding in or near Fort Sumner, and that Garrett, the sheriff, expected that he (Rudolph) would be able to put us on the right trail. Upon my making this statement, Mr. Rudolph apparently became more nervous and excited than ever, and reiterated his reasons for believing that the Kid was not in that part of the country, and showed plainly — so it seemed to me — that he was not only embarrassed but alarmed. The truth was, we afterwards learned, that he was well aware of the fact that the Kid was then, and had been for some time, hiding about Fort Sumner, but his dread of the Kid caused him to make misleading statements while withholding facts.

Darkness was now approaching, and I said to Mr. Rudolph that inasmuch as myself and my horse were by this time pretty well rested, having had a good feed, I had changed my mind, and, instead of stopping overnight with him, would saddle up and ride during the cool of the evening to meet my companions. This I accordingly did, much, I thought, to the relief of Rudolph. I rode directly to the point where I had agreed to meet my companions, and, strange to say, as I approached the point from one direction, they came into view from the other, so that we did not have to wait for each other. This proved to be a night of strange happenings with us, however, all the way through. We here held a consultation as to what further course we should pursue. I had spent the day in endeavoring to learn some-

thing definite of the whereabouts of
the man we wanted, but without
success, save that from the actions of
the people I had met at Fort Sumner,
together with Mr. Rudolph's nervous
and excited manner, I was more
firmly convinced than ever that our
man was in the vicinity.

STRANGE SEQUENCE OF HAPPENINGS
DURING THE NIGHT OF
JULY 14, 1881

Garrett seemed to have but little
confidence in our being able to accomplish the object of our trip, but
said that he knew the location of a
certain house occupied by a woman
in Fort Sumner which the Kid had

The Death of Billy the Kid

formerly frequented, and that if he was in or about Fort Sumner, he would most likely be found entering or leaving this house some time during the night. Garrett proposed that we go into a grove of trees near the town, conceal our horses, then station ourselves in the peach orchard at the rear of the house, and keep watch on who might come or go. This course was agreed upon, and we entered the peach orchard about nine o'clock that night, stationing ourselves in the gloom or shadow of the peach trees, as the moon was shining very brightly. We kept up a fruitless watch here until some time after eleven o'clock, when Garrett stated that he believed we were on a cold trail; that he had very little faith in our being able to accomplish anything when we started on the trip. He proposed that we leave the town without letting anyone know that we had been there in search for the Kid.

I then proposed that, before leaving, we should go to the residence of Peter Maxwell, a man who up to that time I had never seen, but who, by reason of his being a leading citizen and having large property interests, should, according to my reasoning, be glad to furnish such information as he might have to aid us in ridding the country of a man who was looked on as a scourge and curse by all law-abiding people.

Garrett agreed to this, and thereupon led us from the orchard by circuitous by-paths to Maxwell's residence, which was a building formerly used as officers' quarters during the days when a garrison of troops had been maintained at the fort. Upon our arriving at the residence (a very long, one-story adobe, standing end to and flush with the street, having a porch on the south side, which was the direction from which we approached, the premises all being enclosed by a paling fence, one side of which ran parallel to and along the edge of the street up to and across

The Death of Billy the Kid

the end of the porch to the corner of
the building), Garrett said to me,
'This is Maxwell's room in this corner. You fellows wait here while I
go in and talk to him.' Thereupon
he stepped onto the porch and entered Maxwell's room through the
open door (left open on account of
the extremely warm weather), while
McKinney and myself stopped on the
outside. McKinney squatted on the
outside of the fence, and I sat on the
edge of the porch in the small open
gateway leading from the street onto
the porch.

It should be mentioned here that
up to this moment I had never seen
Billy the Kid, nor Maxwell, which

fact, in view of the events transpiring immediately afterward, placed me at an extreme disadvantage.

It was probably not more than thirty seconds after Garrett had entered Maxwell's room, when my attention was attracted, from where I sat in the little gateway, to a man approaching me on the inside of and along the fence, some forty or fifty steps away. I observed that he was only partially dressed and was both bareheaded and barefooted, or rather, had only socks on his feet, and it seemed to me that he was fastening his trousers as he came toward me at a very brisk walk.

As Maxwell's was the one place in

MAXWELL HOUSE

Gate

Room where
Billy was shot

OLD PARADE GROUND

Gate

Room where
Billy left his
coat and boots

Scene of killing of
Billy the Kid

Dotted line
indicates path taken
by the Kid

The Death of Billy the Kid

Fort Sumner that I had considered above suspicion of harboring the Kid, I was entirely off my guard, the thought coming into my mind that the man approaching was either Maxwell or some guest of his who might have been staying there. He came on until he was almost within arm's-length of where I sat, before he saw me, as I was partially concealed from his view by the post of the gate.

Upon his seeing me, he covered me with his six-shooter as quick as lightning, sprang onto the porch, calling out in Spanish, 'Quien es?' (Who is it?) — at the same time backing away from me toward the door

[34]

through which Garrett only a few seconds before had passed, repeating his query, 'Who is it?' in Spanish several times.

At this I stood up and advanced toward him, telling him not to be alarmed, that he should not be hurt; and still without the least suspicion that this was the very man we were looking for. As I moved toward him trying to reassure him, he backed up into the doorway of Maxwell's room, where he halted for a moment, his body concealed by the thick adobe wall at the side of the doorway, from whence he put out his head and asked in Spanish for the fourth or fifth time who I was. I was within a few feet of him when he disappeared into the room.

After this, and until after the shooting, I was unable to see what took place on account of the darkness of the room, but plainly heard what was said on the inside. An instant after the man left the door, I heard a voice inquire in a sharp tone, 'Pete, who are those fellows on the outside?' An instant later a shot was fired in the room, followed immediately by what everyone within hearing distance thought were two other shots. However, there were only two shots fired, the third report, as we learned afterward, being caused by the rebound of the second bullet, which

The Death of Billy the Kid

had struck the adobe wall and re-
bounded against the headboard of
a wooden bedstead.

I heard a groan and one or two
gasps from where I stood in the
doorway, as of someone dying in the
room. An instant later, Garrett came
out, brushing against me as he passed.
He stood by me close to the wall at
the side of the door and said to me,
'That was the Kid that came in there
onto me, and I think I have got him.'
I said, 'Pat, the Kid would not come
to this place; you have shot the wrong
man.'

Upon my saying this, Garrett
seemed to be in doubt himself as
to whom he had shot, but quickly

spoke up and said, 'I am sure that was him, for I know his voice too well to be mistaken.' This remark of Garrett's relieved me of considerable apprehension, as I had felt almost certain that someone whom we did not want had been killed.

A moment after Garrett came out of the door, Pete Maxwell rushed squarely onto me in a frantic effort to get out of the room, and I certainly would have shot him but for Garrett's striking my gun down, saying, 'Don't shoot Maxwell.'

As by this time I had begun to realize that we were in a place which was not above suspicion, such as I had thought the residence of Maxwell to be, and as Garrett was so positive that the Kid was inside, I came to the conclusion that we were up against a case of 'kill or be killed,' such as we had from the beginning realized would be the case whenever we came upon the Kid.

I have ever since felt grateful that I did not shoot Maxwell, for, as I learned afterward, he was at heart a well-meaning, inoffensive man, but very timid. We afterward discovered that the Kid had frequently been at his house after his escape from Lincoln, but Maxwell stood in such terror of him that he did not dare to inform against him.

By this time all was quiet in the

room, and as the darkness was such
that we were unable to see what the
conditions were on the inside or what
the result of the shooting had been,
we — after some rather forceful per-
suasion, indeed — induced Maxwell
to procure a light, which he finally
did by bringing an old-fashioned tal-
low candle from his mother's room
at the far end of the building, pass-
ing by the rear to the end where the
shooting occurred, and placing the
candle on the window-sill from the
outside.

This enabled us to get a view of the
inside, where we saw a man lying
stretched upon his back dead, in the
middle of the room, with a six-shooter

The Death of Billy the Kid

lying at his right hand and a butcher-knife at his left. Upon examining the body, we found it to be that of Billy the Kid. Garrett's first shot had penetrated his breast just above the heart, thus ending the career of a desperado who, while only about twenty-three years of age at the time of his death, had killed a greater number of men than any of the many desperadoes and 'killers' I have known or heard of during the forty-five years I have been in the Southwest.

INQUEST AND BURIAL

Within a very short time after the shooting, quite a number of the native people had gathered around, some of them bewailing the death of their friend, while several women pleaded for permission to take charge of the body, which we allowed them to do. They carried it across the yard to a carpenter shop, where it was laid out on a workbench, the women placing lighted candles around it according to their ideas of properly conducting a 'wake' for the dead.

All that occurred after the Kid came into view in the yard, up to the time he was killed, happened in much less time than it takes to tell it, not more than thirty seconds intervening between the time I first saw him and the time he was shot. From Garrett's statement of what took place in the

room after he entered, it appears that
he left his Winchester rifle standing
by the side of the door, and approached the bed where Maxwell
was sleeping, arousing him and sitting down on the edge of the bed near
the head.

A moment after he had taken this
position for a talk with Maxwell, he
heard voices on the porch and sat
quietly listening, when a man appeared in the doorway and a moment later ran up to Maxwell's bed,
saying, 'Pete, who are those fellows
outside?' It being dark in the room,
he had not up to the moment seen
Garrett sitting at the head of the bed.

When he spoke to Maxwell, Garrett

recognized his voice and made a move to draw his six-shooter. This movement attracted the Kid's attention, and, seeing that a man was sitting there, he instantly covered him with his gun, backed away, and demanded several times in Spanish to know who it was. Garrett made no reply, and, without rising from his seat, fired with the result stated.

This occurred at about midnight on the fourteenth of July, 1881. We spent the remainder of the night on the Maxwell premises, keeping constantly on our guard, as we were expecting to be attacked by the friends of the dead man. Nothing of the kind occurred, however. The next

THE MAXWELL DWELLING-HOUSE AT FORT
SUMNER

THE GRAVE OF BILLY THE KID

The inscription, headed 'Pals,' commemorates Tom
O'Folliard, William Bonney, and Charlie Bowdre. The
grave covered with a concrete mound is that of the Kid.

morning we sent for a justice of the peace, who held an inquest over the body, the verdict of the jury being such as to justify the killing, and, later on the same day, the body was buried in the old military burying ground at Fort Sumner.

CORRECTIONS AND COMMENTS

There have been many wild and untrue stories of this affair, one of which was that we had in some way learned in advance that the Kid would come to Maxwell's residence that night, and had concealed ourselves there with the purpose of waylaying and killing him. Another was that we had cut off fingers and carried them away as trophies or souvenirs, and in later years it has been said many times that the Kid was not dead at all but had been seen alive and well in various places.

The actual facts, however, are exactly as stated herein, and while we no doubt would, under the circumstances, have lain in wait for him at the Maxwell premises if there had been the slightest reason for believing that he would come there, the fact that he did come was a complete surprise to us, absolutely unexpected and unlooked for as far as we three were concerned. The story that we had cut off and carried away his fingers was even more absurd, as the

The Death of Billy the Kid

thought of such a thing never entered our minds, and besides, we were not that kind of people.

The killing of the Kid created a great sensation throughout the Southwest, and many of the law-abiding citizens of New Mexico and the Panhandle contributed substantially and liberally toward a reward for the officers whose work had finally rid the country of a man who was nothing less than a scourge.

The taking-off of the Kid had a very salutary effect in New Mexico and the Panhandle, most of his followers leaving the country, for the time being at least, and a great many persons who had sympathized with

[47]

him or been terrorized by him completely changed their attitude toward
the enforcement of law.

The events which occurred at Maxwell's ranch on the night of that
fourteenth of July to this day seem to
me strange and mysterious, as the
Kid was certainly a 'killer,' was absolutely desperate, and had the drop
first on me and then on Garrett. Why
did he not use it? Possibly because
he thought he was in the house of his
friends and had no suspicion that the
officers of the law would ever come
to that place searching for him. From
what we learned afterward, there
was some reason for believing that we
had been seen leaving the peach or-

chard by one of his friends, who ran to the house where he was stopping for the night, warning him of our presence. Upon which he had run out half-dressed to Maxwell's, thinking that, by reason of the standing of the Maxwell family, he would not be sought there. However this may be, it is still, in view of his character and the condition he was in, a mystery.

I have been in many close places and through many trying experiences both before and after this occurrence, but never in one where I was so forcibly impressed with the idea that a Higher Power controls and rules the destinies of men. To me it seemed

[49]

The Death of Billy the Kid

that what occurred in Fort Sumner
that night had actually been fore-
ordained.

The foregoing sketch or narrative
was written at odd moments, taken
from a very busy business life, upon
the urgent request and oft-repeated
solicitations of friends, and it is the
first — and probably the last — at-
tempt of the writer to record any of
the facts related.

EPILOGUE

As companion to the narrative portion of this book, and supplementing its reference to the formalities of inquest and burial in connection with Billy the Kid, this book may close appropriately with the findings of the coroner's jury. The old document does not seem to have been published hitherto in its entirety, although it has remained for over fifty years among the records in the office of the secretary of the Territory of New Mexico, ever since its arrival as part of the proofs submitted by Pat Garrett to establish his right to the reward offered by Governor Wallace. These

proofs, it happened, had to be un-
usually explicit and convincing, because the new régime, now that Governor Wallace had resigned and Governor Sheldon had been inaugurated,
seemed inclined to withhold payment
of the $500 reward, by taking advan-
tage of a technicality in the wording of
the offer, which seemed to make it a
personal matter on the part of Governor Wallace, instead of an executive
act. To forestall such a contingency,
Pat Garrett with the aid of his lawyer,
Charles W. Green, made a very full
presentation of his claim, and submitted the coroner's verdict in sup-
port of it. The attorney general re-
viewed the matter and reported to

Epilogue

the secretary of the Territory, W. G. Ritch, who seems to have raised the issue, in the absence of Governor Wallace, that the offer might as well be legalized and the money paid to Garrett.

The handwriting of the old document shows that it was composed by the foreman of the coroner's jury, the M. Rudulph referred to in Mr. Poe's story, who was a man of notable education and importance in that section. This fact gives the report more validity than it might have were it simply the record made by those *nativos* whose signatures betray their degree of capability in such a matter. Since the original has the flavor of

Epilogue

the times in being written in Spanish, it is here given in that language as well as in an English translation for those who cannot read Spanish.

TERRITORIO DE NUEVO MÉJICO ⎫
CONDADO DE SAN MIGUEL ⎬ PRECINTO No. 27

Al Procurador del Primer Distrito Judicial del Territorio de Nuevo Méjico
Salud:
   Este dia 15 de Julio, A.D. 1881, reciví
yó, el abajo firmado, Juez de Paz del
Precinto arriba escrito, informacion que
habia habido una muerte en Fuerte
Sumner en dicho precinto é inmediata-
mente al recivir la informacion procedí al
dicho lugar ý nombré á Milnor Rudulph,
José Silva, Antonio Saavedra, Pedro Antonio Lucero, Lorenzo Jaramillo ý Sabal
Gutierres un jurado para averiguar el
asunto ý reuniendose el dicho jurado en
la casa de Luz B. Maxwell procedieron á
un cuarto en dicha casa donde hallaron el
cuerpo de William Bonney alias 'Kid' con

Epilogue

un balazo en el pecho en el lado yzquierdo
del pecho ý habiendo ecsaminado el cuerpo
ecsaminaron la evidencia de Pedro Maxwell
cuya evidencia es como sigue 'Estando yó
acostado en mi cama en mi cuarto a cosa
de media noche el dia 14 de Julio entró á
mi cuarto Pat. F. Garrett ý se sentó en la
orilla de mi cama á platicar conmigo. A
poco rato que Garrett se sentó entró
William Bonney ý se arrimó á mi cama
con una pistola en la mano ý me preguntó
"Who is it? Who is it?" y entónces Pat.
F. Garrett le tiró dos balazos á dicho
William Bonney ý se cayó el dicho Bonney
en un lado de mi fogon ý yó salí del cuarto
cuando volví á entrar yá en tres ó cuatro
minutos despues de los balazos estaba
muerto dicho Bonney.'

El jurado há hallado el siguiente dictámen: 'Nosotros los del jurado unani-
mente hallamos que William Bonney há
sido muerto por un balazo en el pecho
yzquierdo en la region del corazon tirado
de una pistola en la mano de Pat. F. Garrett ý nuestro dictámen es que el hecho de

Epilogue

dicho Garrett fué homicidio justificable
ý estamos unánimes en opinion que la
gratitud de toda la comunidad es devida
á dicho Garrett por su hecho ý que es
digno de ser recompensado.'

M. Rudulph

Presidente

Anto Sabedra

Pedro Anto Lucero

Jose **X** Silba

Sabal **X** Gutierrez

Lorenso **X** Jaramillo

Todo cuya informacion pongo á cono-
cimiento de V.   Alejandro Seguro

Jues de Paz

Territory of New Mexico ⎱ Precinct No. 27
County of San Miguel ⎰

To the Attorney of the First Judicial District of the Territory of New Mexico

Greeting:

This 15th day of July, A.D. 1881, I, the
undersigned, Justice of the Peace of the
Precinct above named, received informa-

Epilogue

tion that there had been a death in Fort
Sumner in said precinct and immediately
on receiving the information I proceeded
to the said place and named Milnor
Rudulph, José Silva, Antonio Saavedra,
Pedro Antonio Lucero, Lorenzo Jaramillo, and Sabal Gutierres a jury to in-
vestigate the matter, and, meeting in the
house of Lucien B. Maxwell, the said jury
proceeded to a room in said house where
they found the body of William Bonney
alias 'Kid' with a bullet wound in the
chest on the left side of the chest, and,
having examined the body, they examined
the evidence of Pedro Maxwell, which
evidence is as follows: 'As I was lying on
my bed in my room about midnight on
the 14th day of July, Patrick F. Garrett
entered my room and sat down on the
edge of my bed to talk with me. Soon after
Garrett had seated himself William Bonney
entered and approached my bed with a
pistol in his hand and asked me, "Who is
it? Who is it?" and then Patrick F. Garrett fired two shots at him, the said William

Epilogue

Bonney, and the said Bonney fell upon one side of my fireplace, and I left the room. When I returned three or four minutes after the shots, the said Bonney was dead.'

The jury has found the following verdict: 'We of the jury unanimously find that William Bonney was killed by a shot in the left breast, in the region of the heart, fired from a pistol in the hand of Patrick F. Garrett, and our verdict is that the act of the said Garrett was justifiable homicide, and we are unanimous in the opinion that the gratitude of the whole community is due to the said Garrett for his act and that he deserves to be rewarded.'

M. RUDULPH
President
ANTO SABEDRA
PEDRO ANTO LUCERO
JOSE X SILBA
SABAL X GUTIERREZ
LORENSO X JARAMILLO

All which information I bring to your notice. ALEJANDRO SEGURO
Justice of the Peace

Epilogue

This report of the coroner's jury shows a feature making it unique among such documents. It is the codicil to the routine findings — 'We are unanimous in the opinion that the gratitude of the whole community is due to the said Garrett for his act and that he deserves to be rewarded.'

This bit of gratuity seems to echo the sigh both of strong relief and ineffable satisfaction which, beginning at Maxwell's ranch, spread through New Mexico and adjacent parts at the realization of their deliverance. Gone now was that young hotblood, typical product and verily a paragon of the bold, reckless life of the frontier, and release had come from the youthful

Epilogue

'bad man' who, if not literally the scourge of the Southwest, had made himself for a brief span of years a general nuisance, not to say an appreciable menace.

MAURICE GARLAND FULTON

FINIS

www.ingramcontent.com/pod-product-compliance
Lightning Source LLC
Chambersburg PA
CBHW032105080426
42733CB00006B/420